SWU-NAP- 023

UNIFORMS OF RUSSIAN ARMY DURING THE NAPOLEONIC WAR VOL.18

UNDER THE REIGN OF ALEXANDER I
EMPEROR OF RUSSIA BETWEEN 1801 AND 1825
GUARDS ARTILLERY, ENGINEERS & GENERAL STAFF

From the Viskovatov's greatest work:
"Historical description of the clothing and
arms of the Russian Army"

English translation by Mark Conrad

SOLDIERSHOP PUBLISHING

AUTHOR

Aleksandr Vasilevich Viskovatov born 22 April (4 May New Style) 1804, died 27 February (11 March) 1858 in St. Petersburg, Russian military historian. He graduated from the 1st Cadet Corps and served in the artillery, the hydrographic depot of the Naval Ministry, and then in the Department of Military Educational Institutions. He mainly studied historical artifacts and the histories of military units. Viskovatov's greatest work was the Historical Description of the Clothing and Arms of the Russian Army.

PUBLISHING'S NOTE

NOTE ABOUT BOOK PRINTING BEFORE 1925

LICENSES COMMONS

ACKNOWLEDGEMENTS

A Special Thanks to NYPL and other institutions for their kindly permission to use some images of his archives, collections or books used in our book.

Title: **UNIFORMS OF RUSSIAN ARMY DURING THE NAPOLEONIC WAR VOL. 18**
Guards artillery, Engineers & General Staff By A.V.Viskovatov. Serie edit by Luca S. Cristini. First edition by Soldiershop. May 2018 Cover & Art Design: Luca S. Cristini. Plates re-colorations by Anna Cristini. ISBN code: 978-88-93273466

Published by Soldiershop publishing, via Padre Davide, 7 - 24050 Zanica (BG) ITALY. wwwsoldiershop.com

UNIFORMS OF THE RUSSIAN ARMY DURING THE NAPOLEONIC WAR VOL. 18

UNDER THE REIGN OF ALEXANDER I EMPEROR OF
RUSSIA BETWEEN 1801 AND 1825

*

GUARDS ARTILLERY, ENGINEERS & ROYAL STAFF

ALEXANDRE PREMIER.

Pleurons et gémissons, Alexandre n'est plus!
Sort cruel! C'est en vain que l'univers t'implore,
Ah! si tu respectois les plus belles vertus,
Alexandre vivroit encore.

Mais le ciel appaisé, donnant à Nicolas
Et ses rares vertus, et sa belle Couronne,
Dissipe nos terreurs; il prouve qu'il est las
De punir, et qu'il nous pardonne.

Louis Bosis invenit   1826   Alexander Flers fecit.

HISTORICAL DESCRIPTION OF THE CLOTHING AND ARMS OF THE RUSSIAN ARMY - A.V. VISKOVATOV
(First English translation by Mark Conrad)

Soldiershop is glad to presents the complete collection of the great job made by A.V. Viskovatov dedicated to the uniforms and weapons belonging to the Russian army during the Napoleonic period, until 1825. The time we considered corresponds to the reigns of two Tzars: Paul I, who reigned since 1769 until his murder on the 23rd of March 1801, and his son Aleksandr Pavlovič Romanov, that with the title of Alexander I, sat on the throne until the 1st December 1825.

Our reprint in based on the original 19th century volumes, to be precise the volumes from 7 to 9 are dedicated to the reign of Paul I; this first part is distributed on 7 volumes, having a numbering from 1 to 7. From number 10 to 18 of the original volumes, the second part is dedicated to the Russian troops under Alexander I. These still being worked on and they will be soon ready, distributed on twenty volumes approximately. Our new edition, the first ever published in English, both on paper and digital format, boasts a large number of color plates, many of them unpublished and coloured by our team of expert artists and scholars of uniformology. Each volume is based on 50/70 plates, always accompanied by the original translated text which describes the uniforms, the organization and the armament of the Russian army of the period.

In this book we present the Russian Guards artillery, Engineers and general Staff of the Napoleonic wars.

A unique work in its genre, a must have in any respecting collection!

Aleksandr Vasilevich Viskovatov born 22 April (4 May New Style) 1804, died 27 February (11 March) 1858 in St. Petersburg, Russian military historian. He graduated from the 1st Cadet Corps and served in the artillery, the hydrographic depot of the Naval Ministry, and then in the Department of Military Educational Institutions. He mainly studied historical artifacts and the histories of military units. Viskovatov's greatest work was the Historical Description of the Clothing and Arms of the Russian Army (Vols. 1-30, St. Petersburg, 1841-62; 2nd ed. Vols. 1-34, St. Petersburg - Novosibirsk - Leningrad, 1899-1948). This work is based on a great quantity of archival documents and contains four thousand colored illustrations.

Viskovatov was the author of Chronicles of the Russian Army (Books 1-20, St. Petersburg, 1834-42) and Chronicles of the Russian Imperial Army (Parts 1-7, St. Petersburg, 1852). He collected valuable material on the history of the Russian navy which went into A Short Overview of Russian Naval Campaigns and General Voyages to the End of the XVII Century (St. Petersburg, 1864; 2nd edition Moscow, 1946). Together with A.I. Mikhailovskii-Danilevskii he helped prepare and create the Military Gallery in the Winter Palace.

He wrote the historical military inscriptions for the walls of the Hall of St. George in the Great Palace of the Kremlin. (From the article in the Soviet Military Encyclopedia.)

◀ *Alexander of Russia in a contemporary print*

CONTENTS

*

Preface pag. 5

*

RUSSIAN ARMY- GUARDS ARTILLERY

CHANGES IN THE UNIFORMS AND EQUIPMENT OF GUARDS ARTILLERY, SAPPERS, ENGINEERS,
HORSE PIONEERS, GENERAL STAFF FROM 1801 TO 1825.

XLI. GUARDS FOOT ARTILLERY. *[Gvardeiskaya peshaya artilleriya.]*

9 April 1801 - Lower ranks of the foot companies in the L.-Gds. Artillery Battalion were ordered to cut off their curls [*pukli*] and have **queues** [*kosy*] only 4 vershoks [7 inches] long, tying them midway down the collar [1].

10 May 1801 - **Train officers** [*furshtatskie ofitsery*] in the L.-Gds. Artillery Battalion were prescribed to have the uniforms as other officers in this battalion, except with green pants [2].

18 May 1801 - Lower combatant ranks of the foot companies in the **L.-Gds. Artillery Battalion** were given dark-green coats. These were of the same pattern as prescribed at this time for lower combatant ranks of Army and Guards Infantry, with a collar and cuffs of black worsted velvet [*trip*] or black plissé [*plis*]. There were flaps on the cuffs and—for gun handlers [*gandlangery*], cannoneers, and bombardiers—also a strap on the left shoulder, of black cloth with red cloth piping. There was the same sewn-on tape on the collar and cuff flaps as in the L.-Gds. Preobrazhenskii Regiment. The skirt turnbacks were of black cloth trimmed with red cloth piping, and the lining was black kersey (Illus. 2138). Small clothes were of pale straw-colored cloth. The hat tassels were yellow with a dark-green center. Boots, with a a notch cut out in the back, and all other items of clothing, accouterments, and arms were prescribed to be as for Army Foot Artillery, except that buttons, sword hilts, short-sword hooks and chapes, and metal fittings to sword belts, powder holders, crossbelts, and knapsack straps were all of copper (red brass) as for the rest of the Guards. Also, the crossbelt for drummers was trimmed with yellow and red tape. Officers had gold embroidered buttonhole loops on the coat's collar and cuff flaps, and a gold aiguilette on the right shoulder. Otherwise, they were distinguished from lower ranks in the same way as throughout the Infantry, except that they were not authorized gorgets (Illus. 2138) [3].

11 June 1801 - **Small clothes** for all combatant ranks, as well as the **gloves** of non-commissioned officers and officers, were ordered to be white instead of the previous pale straw color (Illus. 2138) [4].

27 October 1802 - Generals and field and company-grade officers, when on the march with troops or on detached duties, were ordered to wear, instead of white pants, **gray riding trousers** with brass buttons and leather reinforcement, identical to those established at this time for generals and field and company-grade officers of Army and Guards Infantry and Cavalry [5].

16 June 1803 - The small clothes of officers of the **train** [*furshtatskie ofitsery*] was ordered to be gray instead of green [6].

29 June 1803 - Generals and field and company-grade officers were ordered to have the same **shabracks** and **pistol carriers** as given at this time to generals and field and company-grade officers of Army Foot Artillery, but with velvet inlay instead of cloth, and with the addition of silver Guards stars (Illus. 2139) [7].

19 August 1803 - Lower ranks were given cloth **headdresses** in place of hats, of the same pattern as received on 19 October 1804 by the L.-Gds. Preobrazhenskii, Semenovskii, and Izmailovskii Regiments, but without plumes. These had the same two small tassels as were on the hat, i.e. yellow outside and dark green in the middle (Illus. 2140 and 2141) [8].

17 December 1803 - Confirmation was given to a new **table of uniforms, accouterments, and weapons** for the L.-Gds. Artillery Battalion, based on which the lower ranks of its foot companies kept all their previous uniform clothing and arms, with only the removal of red piping from cuff flaps. Around this time field and company-grade officers began to wear **hats** with a buttonhole loop made from thin gold galloon instead of being embroidered, and with a tall plume, as already mentioned above for officers of Army and Guards Infantry and Cavalry (Illus. 2142) [9].

4 January 1805 - The round **powder flasks** [*porokhovyya natruski*] used by bombardiers, cannoneers, and gun handlers were replaced by **pouches** [*lyadunki ili podsumkami*] of the same pattern as that introduced at this time for Army Foot Artillery, except with a badge of copper ["red brass"] (Illus. 2143) [10].

1 October 1806 - The sheepskin **warm coats** [*ovchinnyya fufaiki*] and **short coats** [*polushubki*] authorized for lower ranks up to now were withdrawn [11], and about this time HIGHEST Confirmation was given to rules drawn up under the direct supervision of the then Inspector of All Artillery, General Graf Arakcheev, regarding the sewing, cut, fitting, and wear of lower ranks' **uniforms** and **accouterments**. These rules, set forth above under Army Foot Artillery, were extended with equal force to foot companies of the L.-Gds. Artillery Battalion [12].

10 March 1807- Canes were withdrawn for officers [13].

17 September 1807 - Generals and field and company-grade officers were ordered to wear a gold **epaulette** on the left shoulder, of the pattern established for the rest of the Guards, and on the right shoulder—a gold aiguilette, as before (Illus. 2144) [14]. From this year onward these ranks stopped wearing **queues** and continued to powder their hair only for grand parades and appearances at HIGHEST Court. For lower ranks **hair** powder was completely eliminated and queues cut off short [15].

26 September and 19 December 1807 - Lower ranks were ordered to wear **sword belts** not around the waist, but over the right shoulder, as would be introduced on 7 March 1808 for Army Foot Artillery (Illus. 2145) [16].

23 December 1807 - Lower ranks were given new pattern summer and winter **pants** of the pattern confirmed at this same time for Army and Guards Infantry, i.e. the former with spats and the latter with leather trim or leggings [*kragi*], with seven brass buttons. Company-grade officers when in summer uniform were ordered to wear the same pants as lower ranks, and in winter—boots reaching to under the knee, without any cutout behind short [17].

3 January 1808 - Private lower ranks were ordered to have to have red shoulder straps on both shoulders. **Pompons** on the regulation headdress were to be white with a red center (Illus. 2145), and the the loop above the tassel on forage caps and the ring and loop of the sword knot were to be according to the company: in the first battery company - white, in the second battery company - red, in the first light company - sky blue, and in the second light company - green [18].

26 January 1808 - Generals at parades, on designated calendar days [*tabelnye dni*], and at troop formations in general, in peacetime as well as during wartime, were ordered to wear the newly introduced standard **generals' coat** [*obshchii generalskii mundir*]. And with the coat of the Guards Foot Artillery, when not on duty, they were to have dark-green pants instead of white [19].

(Note: A description of the standard general-officer's coat is located below, at the end of the treatment of EMPEROR ALEXANDER I's reign, in the chapter on generals' uniforms.)

16 April 1808 - Privates and field and company-grade officers of foot companies in the Guards Artillery were given **shakos** [*kivera*] of the same pattern as established at this time for the L.-Gds. Preobrazhenskii, Semenovskii, and Izmailovskii Regiments, but without a plume and with a different pattern of front plate, one depicting a two-headed eagle sitting on two crossed cannons, below which lay various artillery munitions (Illus. 2146, 2147, and 2148) [20].

14 July 1808 - The round **knapsacks** used by lower ranks were exchanged for rectangular ones of the same pattern as those received at this time by Army and Guards Heavy Infantry and Army Artillery. Along with this, it was set forth as a rule that when the **greatcoat** was not being worn it was to be carried in accordance with same directives as described above in detail under grenadier uniforms (Illus. 2146) [21].

28 November 1808 [sic, should be 2 November - M.C.] - The winter **pants** with leather cuffs and the summer ones with spats, authorized on 23 December 1807, were kept only for combatant lower ranks, while for noncombatants the pants as well as the boots were ordered to be of the old patterns, i.e. the latter halfway up the calf [*v pol ikry*], with a cutout in the back [22].

5 November 1808 - Company-grade officers, when the troops were wearing **knapsacks**, were ordered to also have them, of the same pattern in all respects as was established for lower ranks (Illus. 2147) [23].

12 November 1808 - Field and company-grade officers, when not on duty, were allowed to wear dark-green **pants** instead of white [24].

27 March 1809 - Instead of one **epaulette**, generals and field and company-grade officers were ordered to wear two, and consequently the aiguilettes which had been in use were abolished (Illus. 2148) [25]. Around this same time these personnel began to wear on their dress coats, instead of buttonhole loops, the newly established gold **embroidery** (Illus. 2149) [26].

4 April 1809 - **Noncommissioned officers** were ordered to have galloon not on the lower and side edges of the collar, but on the upper and side edges [27].

20 April 1809 - The change in the manner of wearing the **knapsack**, introduced at this time throughout the Infantry and described above in detail for Grenadier regiments as well as the L.-Gds. Preobrazhenskii, Semenovskii, and Izmailovskii Regiments, i.e. with the addition of a third chest strap, was extended to foot companies of the Guards Artillery (Illus. 2150) [28].

24 May 1809 - Field and company-grade officers of the Guards Foot Artillery were given **gorgets** [*znaki*] of the same pattern as those established at this time for the L.-Gds. Izmailovskii Regiment (Illus. 2151) [29].

8 June 1809 - The plumage on **generals' hats** was discontinued. The hat's former pattern of embroidered buttonhole was replaced with a new one made of four thick, twisted cords, of which the two middle ones were intertwined with each other as if in a plait (Illus. 2151) [30].

11 June 1809 - Combatant lower ranks were ordered to have red **shako cords** and **pompons** (Illus. 2152), while for non-commissioned officers the cords were to be multicolored, i.e. white, black, and orange, with the pompon as before: two quarters white and two black with orange (Illus. 2152) [31].

6 December 1809 - Instead of the former fine chain on the **shako**, field and company-grade officers were ordered to flat scales, as established at this time for officers of Guards Infantry (Illus. 2153) [32]. In this same year any **hair powder** still being used by generals and officers was abolished, and they were allowed to wear **frock coats** of the same pattern as received by officers of Army Artillery, except with a velvet collar and without red piping [33].

10 February 1810 - Instead of a single chin strap, lower ranks' **shakos** were given two chin straps with flat copper chin-scales (Illus. 2154). Officers were ordered to have completely silver shako cords without any addition of black or orange silk, and to shorten the plumes on their hats (Illus. 2155) [34].

24 September 1810 - The **knapsack** straps for lower ranks were ordered to be stitched at the edges, in the manner of cross-belts and sword belts, and have a bend at each shoulder so that they do not wear away the coat and are not constricting under the arms [35].

17 January 1811 - Instead of the multicolored cords on their **shakos**, noncommissioned officers and musicians were ordered to have red ones, the cords' tassels being white with black and orange mixed in (Illus. 2156) [36].

25 October 1811 - Combatant lower ranks were given a new pattern of **forage cap**, identical to that established at this time for Army Foot Artillery (Illus. 2156) [37].

3 November 1811 - **Gloves** were discontinued for non-commissioned officers, and in their place in cold weather they were allowed to wear cloth mittens sewn from old tailcoats, as done at this time for privates [38]. Also, from this year forward non-commissioned officers stopped carrying **canes** [39].

In January 1812 - All combatant ranks were ordered to have **shakos** and **collars** of a new style, lower than previously. The first item had a greater spread or widening toward the top and concave sides, and the second was closed in front and had red cloth piping around it. At this time red piping was also added to cuffs and cuff flaps (Illus. 2157). Along with these changes, lower ranks were given integral **leggings** [*kragi*] reaching up to the knees, with nine buttons instead of seven, and the previous sewn-on **tape** on the coats, with a checked design, was replaced with sewn-on buttonhole loops made from yellow woolen tape with orange stripes. This tape was also used to trim the coats of musicians and drummers. There was a red light, or thin stripe, on this tape, and a black light on the buttonhole loops on the collar and cuff flaps (Illus. 2157) [40]. The change in collar pattern as described here, there was a change in the gold **embroidery** on officers' coats, consisting of the loop's slanted aspect becoming straightened so as to conform to the collar's new upright edges (Illus. 2157).

10 February 1812 - Lower noncombatant ranks were given the same **uniform** as prescribed on this date for regiments of Guards Infantry, but with black piping and red shoulder straps (Illus. 2158) [41].

20 May 1814 - For campaign use, officers were ordered to change their previous **riding trousers** [*reituzy*] with leather re-inforcements and buttons to ones without leather and buttons, with two wide stripes of black cloth along the outer side seams, and on the seams themselves—piping of red cloth (Illus. 2159) [42].

28 May 1814 - All combatant ranks were given hair **plumes** for their shakos, black for privates and officers, red for drummers, and for personnel holding non-commissioned officer rank—with a white top with a longitudinal yellow stripe, similar to the existing distinction in Army and Guards Infantry (Illus. 2159 and 2160) [43]. In this same year it was ordered to have white tape around the **cockades** on officers' hats, which later became silver. In 1815 uniforms for **drum majors** were introduced, identical to those prescribed at this time for drum majors in regiments of the Old Guard [44].

22 December 1815 - White cloth **pants** were withdrawn for all combatant ranks, and dark-green pants were to be worn at all times [45].

24 January 1816 - The **scabbards** for lower ranks' short swords [*tesaki*] and officers' rapiers [*shpagi*] were ordered to be black and lacquered [46].

12 May 1817 - With the formation of the 1st and 2nd L.-Gds. Artillery Brigades from the single **L.-Gds. Artillery Brigade**, their combatant personnel were ordered to have black turnbacks or lapels [*otvoroty ili latskany*] on their dress coats (velvet for officers, plissé for lower ranks), with red cloth piping. The brigades were distinguished from each other by their cuff flaps: 1st Brigade - red (Illus. 2161, 2162, and 2163); 2nd Brigade - dark green with red piping (Illus. 2164 and 2165) [47]. Besides this, the 2nd Brigade followed the example of the 2nd Guards Infantry Division's regiments (Moscow, Grenadier, Pavlovsk, and Finland) in being given for their greatcoat collars red cloth patches with a brass button (gilt for officers) (Illus. 2166) [48]. The first battery companies of both brigades received sword knots with a red tassel, the second battery companies with a white tassel, and the light companies a blue [*svetlosinii*] knot [49].

13 May 1817 - In order to relieve combatant lower ranks while on campaign and to protect their accouterments, it was laid down that during such times they were always to be in greatcoats and that their shako, plume, pouch, and uniform with leggings were to have **covers** [*chekhly*] of raven's-duck or Flemish linen painted with black oil paint, in all respects according to the instructions set forth on this subject at this same time for all Army and Guards Infantry and Army Foot Artillery [50].

8 August 1817 - The size of the **forage cap** was laid down as described above in detail for Grenadier regiments [51].

26 September 1817 - The description of **accouterments** and the instructions for the manner of wearing them in the Guards heavy infantry, issued on this date, was extended with equal force to the Guards Foot Artillery [52].

8 December 1817 - It was ordered that for lower ranks the leather cuffs on cloth **pants** were to have spat-like projections [*kozyr'ki*] of a pattern similar to the spats on summer pants [53].

2 March 1818 - The newly established **L.-Gds. Foot Battery Company No. 5** in Warsaw was prescribed to have the same uniform as the L.-Gds. 1st Artillery Brigade, but with black cloth spats (for lower ranks) instead of leather pants cuffs (Illus. 2167), and an image of a Lithuanian horseman on the shako plate's shield and on officers' gorgets. Also, field-grade officers were ordered to not wear *bottes fortes* [*botforty*] as in the two Guards Artillery brigades, but the **boots** of company-grade officers that only reached to the knees, with spurs (Illus. 2168) [54].

21 March 1818 - In order to be distinguished from L.-Gds. Battery Company No. 5, the coats of the **L.-Gds. 1st Artillery Battery** were ordered to have white cloth piping on the cuff flaps (Illus. 2169) [55].

23 August 1818 - The length and width of **shoulder straps** on tailcoats and greatcoats was defined, identical to that laid down at this time for Army and Guards Infantry and described above in detail for Grenadier regiments [56]. It was also confirmed that musicians' and drummers' coats would have red shoulder wings or swallows' nests [*plechevye klapany ili kryl'tsa*] [57].

25 January 1819 - **Drumsticks** and the handles of **entrenching tools** were ordered to be be yellow [58].

4 April 1819 - For lower ranks in the 1st and 2nd Brigades the spats on the **leggings** were removed [59].

20 September 1820 - Field and company-grade officers throughout the Guards Foot Artillery were given a new pattern **gorget**, identical to that established at this time for Guards Infantry regiments, but without the inscription "1700 NO 19" as in the Preobrazhenskii and Semenovskii Regiments (Illus. 2170). In the companies of the 1st and 2nd Brigades there was, on the eagle's shield on these gorgets, an image of St. George, as previously, and for the L.-Gds. Battery Company

No. 5 the image of a Lithuanian horseman was kept [60]. In this same year the **sewn-on chevrons** on the coats of musicians and drummers began to be placed closer together, almost touching one another, and on the swallows' nests the tape was no longer perpendicular as before, but at a diagonal toward the lower edge. Also, all four sides of the collar began to be trimmed with this tape (Illus. 2171) [61].

26 November 1823 - All **musicians**, even though they might not hold non-commissioned officer ranks, were ordered to have: gold galloon on the coat and non-commisied officers' pompons on the shakos. This did not apply to drummers if they did not hold non-commissioned officer rank [62].

16 January 1824 - The following changes were ordered in the uniforms and accouterments of combatant lower ranks:

1) **Coattails**, which up to this time had one covering the other, were to be cut so that their inner edges came together, and sewn together where they touched (Illus. 2172).

2.) To the decorative end [*trinchik*] of the **shako cords**, which was to be level with the right shoulder, was to be added a special loop of white cord attached to the button on the right shoulder strap, so that the shako cords would stay in place when the soldier moved about (Illus. 2172).

3.) The **knapsack** chest strap was to be fitted so that it passed between the third and fourth buttons of the coat, as counted from the bottom (Illus. 2172) [63].

From this year, officers as well as lower ranks began to wear a taller **shako** with wider cords (Illus. 2172 and 2173), but no regulations were issued in this regard [64].

29 March 1825 - For combatant lower ranks, for faultless service, there were established **stripes** [*nashivki*] to be sewn on the left sleeve: for 10 years service - one, for 15 years - two, for 20 years - three; one over the other, all of yellow tape [65].

XLII. GUARDS HORSE ARTILLERY. *[Gvardeiskaya konnaya artilleriya.]*

9 April 1801 - Lower ranks of the L.-Gds. Artillery Battalion's Horse company were ordered to cut off their curls [*pukli*] and have **queues** [*kosy*] only 4 vershoks [7 inches] long, tying them midway down the collar [66].

10 May 1801 - **Train officers** [*furshtatskie ofitsery*] in the L.-Gds. Artillery Battalion's Horse company were prescribed to have the uniforms as other officers in this battalion, except with green pants [67].

18 May 1801 - The L.-Gds. Artillery Battalion's Horse company was the same uniforms as the battalion's foot companies, but with the addition of a yellow worsted **aiguilette** for lower ranks (Illus. 2174). Other other pieces of uniform, accouterments, and weaponry were prescribed to be the same as for Army Horse Artillery, except for yellow brass being replaced by **copper** (red brass) (Illus. 2174) [68].

11 June 1801 - **Small clothes** for all combatant ranks, as well as the **gloves** of non-commissioned officers and officers, were ordered to be white instead of the previous pale straw color [69].

27 October 1802 - Generals and field and company-grade officers, when on the march with troops or on detached duties, were ordered to wear, instead of white pants, gray **riding trousers** with brass buttons and leather reinforcement, identical to those established at this time for generals and field and company-grade officers of Army and Guards Infantry and Cavalry [71].

16 June 1803 - The **small clothes** of officers of the train [*furshtatskie ofitsery*] was ordered to be gray instead of green [72].

18 October 1803 - All combatant ranks were given **helmets** instead of hats, of the same pattern as those introduced at this time in the Cavalier Guards and Horse regiments (Illus. 2176, 2177, 2178, and 2179) [73].

17 December 1803 - Bombardiers and cannoneers were ordered to have two **pistols** instead of one [74], and a new pattern of **saddlecloth** was confirmed, of dark-green cloth: for lower ranks—with one row of the same tape as on the coat, and with a straw-colored cloth monogram of EMPEROR ALEXANDER I and crown (Illus. 2176), and for officers—with one row of gold galloon and silver stars of the standard Guards pattern (Illus. 2179) [75]. Around this time generals and field and company-grade officers began to wear **hats** with a with a tall plume. The field and company-grade officers also had a buttonhole loop of narrow gold galloon instead of embroidery (Illus. 2180) [76].

27 February 1804 - The deerskin **pants** prescribed for the Guards Horse Artillery were replaced by white cloth pants [77].

1 October 1806 - The sheepskin **warm coats**, or short coats [*ovchinnyya fufaiki, ili polushubki*], authorized for lower ranks up to now were withdrawn [78], and about this time HIGHEST Confirmation was given to rules drawn up under the direct supervision of the then Inspector of All Artillery, General Graf Arakcheev, regarding the sewing, cut, fitting, and wear of lower ranks' **uniforms and accouterments**. These rules, set forth above under Army Horse Artillery, were extended with equal force to Horse companies of the L.-Gds. Artillery Battalion, which from this time received white (instead of the previous dark green) **forage caps** with a red band and a tassel colored white and red (Illus. 2181) [79].

10 March 1807- **Canes** were withdrawn for officers [80].

17 September 1807 - Generals and field and company-grade officers were ordered to wear a gold **epaulette** on the left shoulder, of the pattern established for the rest of the Guards, and on the right shoulder—a gold aiguilette, as before (Illus. 2182) [81]. From this year onward these ranks stopped wearing **queues** and continued to powder their hair only for grand parades and appearances at HIGHEST Court. For lower ranks hair powder was completely eliminated and queues cut off short [82].

3 January 1808 - **Shoulder straps** in the Guards Horse Artillery, instead of black worsted velvet or plissé [*chernye tripovye, ili plisovye*] with red piping, were ordered to be red cloth (Illus. 2183) [83].

26 January 1808 - Generals at parades, on designated calendar days [*tabelnye dni*], and at troop formations in general, in peacetime as well as during wartime, are ordered to wear the newly introduced standard **generals' coat** [*obshchii generalskii mundir*]. And with the coat of the Guards Horse Artillery, when not on duty, they are to have dark-green pants instead of white [84].

26 November 1808 - The L.-Gds. Horse Artillery is ordered to have **plumes** on their helmets in the new flat style—black for officers, non-commissioned officers, and privates, and red for musicians. The helmets are also given **chinstraps** with flat scales (Illus. 2183 and 2184). Officers are ordered to wear such helmets only when on campaign, and during the rest of the time they are to have the previous—i.e. thick and dense—plumes [85].

27 March 1809 - Instead of one **epaulette**, generals and field and company-grade officers are ordered to wear two, and consequently the aiguilettes which had been in use are abolished [86]. Around this same time these ranks began to wear on their dress coats, instead of buttonhole loops, the newly established gold **embroidery**, the same as was given to officers of Guards Foot Artillery (Illus. 2185) [87].

4 April 1809 - **Non-commissioned officers** are ordered to have galloon not on the lower and side edges of the coat collar, but on the upper and side edges [88].

8 June 1809 - The **plumage** on generals' hats is discontinued. The hat's former pattern of embroidered buttonhole is replaced with a new one made of four thick, twisted cords, of which the two middle ones are intertwined with each other as if in a plait [89].

22 October 1809 - All lower ranks are ordered to have two **shoulder straps**, colored red as before, while the aiguilettes were taken away (Illus. 2186) [90]. In this same year the **hair powder** still being used by generals and officers was abolished, and they were allowed to wear **frock coats** of the same pattern as received by officers of Guards Foot Artillery, except with white lining [91].

2 February 1811 - The Guards Horse Artillery is ordered to have:

1) **Shakos** instead of helmets, the same as for Guards Foot Artillery but with a white hair plume (red for trumpeters), at whose root was black hair with an admixture of orange. Personnel holding non-commissioned officer rank were distinguished by a black and orange top (Illus. 2187 and 2188).

2) Instead of white pants with hight boots—long dark-green **pants** or **chakchiry trousers** with red inserts or stripes and the same color of piping, following the pattern for lancer chakchiry, and the boots as lancers (Illus. 2187 and 2188).

3) Instead of broad swords—**sabers** of the same pattern as for lancers (Illus. 2187 and 2188).

4) On lower ranks' **saddlecloths**, instead of one row of red with yellow checks—two rows of yellow tape without checks, sewn along a black insert piped red (Illus. 2187) [92].

25 October 1811 - Combatant lower ranks are given a new pattern of **forage cap**, identical to that receieved at this time by the Guards Foot Artillery [93]. Also, in this year non-commissioned officers' **canes** were withdrawn [94].

In **January 1812** - The Guards Horse Artillery underwent the same changes in uniforms as occurred at this time in the Guards Foot Artillery, i.e. **collars** were lower than before and no longer open in front at an angle but rather closed with small hooks, red cloth piping was added around the collar and to the coat's cuffs, and the tape on lower ranks' dress coats was changed (Illus. 2189 and 2190) [95].

10 February 1812 - Lower noncombatant ranks are given new **uniforms**, the same as established on this date for lower noncombatant ranks in the Guards Foot Artillery [96].

20 May 1814 - Officers on campaign are ordered to have the same **riding trousers** [*reituzy*] as given at this time to the Guards Foot Artillery, but with red stripes instead of black (Illus. 2191) [97].

26 June 1814 - All combatant ranks are ordered to have **single-breasted coats** instead of double-breasted, with nine buttons (Illus. 2191 and 2912) [98]. Also, beginning this year, white lace was added around the cockades on officers' **hats**, the lace later being changed to silver [99].

7 March 1816 - Officers are ordered to sew gold galloon onto the **sword belts** for their sabers (Illus. 2194) [100].

19 March 1817 - It is ordered that only officers and non-commissioned officers were to have **gloves**, in both cases without gauntlet cuffs [101].

12 May 1817 - The Guards Horse Artillery, at this time consisting of three batteries (Battery and Light Nos. 1 and 2) is ordered to have **dress coats** with red cloth cuff flaps and the same lapels as were given at this time to the Guards Foot Artillery, i.e. black (plissé for lower ranks and velvet for officers), with red piping (Illus. 2193 and 2194) [102].

25 May 1817 - Field and company-grade officers, when in formation and parades, are ordered to have **coats** with short tails and wear these with **cartridge pouches** on crossbelts with gold galloon and silver fittings (Illus. 2194 and 2195) [103].

2 March 1818 - The newly established L.-Gds. Horse Artillery Light Battery No. 3 in Warsaw is prescribed to have the same uniform as the preceding three batteries, but with an image of a Lithuanian horseman on the shako plate's shield instead of St. George, and an oblong pompon the same color as the shako cords, instead of a plume (Illus. 2196) [104].

18 March 1818 - This battery is ordered to have dark-green **cuff flaps** with red piping (Illus. 2196), while those in the first three batteries remained all red [105].

21 March 1818 - The same three batteries are ordered to have white piping on their red **cuff flaps** (Illus. 2197) [106].

16 February 1819 - The Guards Horse Artillery is ordered to have **covers** on shakos and plumes, identical to those established at this time for Dragoon, Hussar, and Horse-Jäger regiments and Army Horse Artillery [107].

23 April 1820 - The first three batteries are ordered to have, instead of plumes, the same oblong **pompons** as in Light Battery No. 3 (Illus. 2198) [108]. In this same year the sewn-on **chevrons** on the trumpeters' coats began to be placed closer together, almost touching one another, and on the swallows' nests the tape was no longer perpendicular as before, but at a diagonal toward the lower edge. Also, all four sides of the **collar** began to be trimmed with this tape [109].

1 May 1824 - It is ordered to have round **pompons** instead of oblong (Illus. 2199) [110]. In this same year all combatant ranks began to wear a taller **shako** with wider cords. The latter had a special loop to attach to the button of the right shoulder strap (Illus. 2199) [111].

29 March 1825 - For combatant lower ranks, for faultless service, there are established **stripes** [*nashivki*] to be sewn on the left sleeve: for 10 years service - one, for 15 years - two, for 20 years - three; one over the other, all of yellow tape [112].

XLIII . GUARDS SAPPERS. [*Gvardeiskie sapery.*]

27 December 1812 - The newly formed **L.-Gds. Sapper Battalion**, consisting of two Miner and two Sapper companies, is given the exact same uniforms and weapons as Army Sapper and Pioneer regiments had at this time, but with black plissé collars and cuffs (black velvet for officers) with guards tape sewn on for lower ranks, and for officers—the same embroidery as in Guards Artillery but in silver. Pouches had the round guards pattern badge in copper, and there was a guards pattern badge on the shako with two crossed axes beneath it. A further distinction is that pants were not gray, but dark green (Illus. 2200, 2201, and 2202). Officers' shabracks and pistol carriers in this battalion are the same as in Guards Foot Artillery but with silver galloon instead of gold [113].

20 Mary 1814 - The campaign **riding trousers** of gray cloth with buttons and leather reinforcement on the inner seams, used by officers since the establishment of the battalion, are withdrawn, and in their place were given the same riding trousers as received at this time by officers throughout the Foot Artillery and in Army Sapper and Pioneer regiments, i.e. with wide black stripes and red piping [114].

31 July 1814 - The **pistols** given to miners since the time the battalion was established are withdrawn and replaced by **dragoon muskets** [*dragunskiya ruzh'ya*], i.e. the same as in the Sapper companies (Illus. 2203) [115]. In this same year white tape was added around the **cockades** on officers' hats, later replaced by silver. In 1815 uniforms for **drum majors** were established, identical to those prescribed at this time for drum majors in the rest of the Old Guard [116].

24 and 27 January 1816 - The **scabbards** for lower ranks' short swords [*tesaki*] and officers' rapiers [*shpagi*] are ordered to be black and lacquered, and lower ranks' shako cords were to be white instead of red [117].

5 March 1816 - All combatant ranks are ordered to add red piping to the lower edge of the **collar**, after the example of the Guards Artillery [118].

9 March 1816 - HIGHEST Confirmation is given to a new table of uniforms, accouterments, and other items for the L.-Gds. Sapper Battalion, based on which it keeps its previous uniform clothing and arms. Only new **shakos** are issued, taller than before, with a flat top instead of the concave pattern prescribed since 1812 (Illus. 2204, 2205, and 2206). Also, in each Sapper company, for use during training exercises, black iron **helmets** and **cuirasses** are authorized for one officer, one non-commissioned officer, and four sappers. For miners, in case they had to carry out mining work during wartime, it is ordered that one pistol be kept for each man, after the example of Army Sapper and Pioneer battalions, as described above [119].

23 May 1816 - Field and company-grade officers are given **gorgets** of the same pattern as used by Guards Infantry and Guards Foot Artillery (Illus. 2206) [120].

8 May 1817 - All combatant ranks are ordered to have a red cloth tab on each side of the **greatcoat collar**, with a button on each tab, as related above for regiments of the 2nd Guards Infantry Division and for the 2nd Guards Artillery Brigade [121].

12 May 1817- Black **lapels** are added to the dress coats of the L.-Gds. Sapper Battalion. For lower ranks these were of plissé, and for officers—of velvet, in both cases with red cloth piping (Illus. 2207 and 2208) [122].

13 May 1817 - In order to relieve combatant lower ranks while on campaign and to protect their accouterments, it is laid down that during such times they were always to be in greatcoats and that their shako, plume, pouch, and uniform with leggings were to have **covers** [*chekhly*] of raven's-duck or Flemish linen painted with black oil paint, in all respects according to the instructions set forth on this subject at this same time for all Army and Guards Infantry [123].

8 August 1817 - The size of the **forage cap** is laid down as described above in detail for Grenadier regiments [124].

26 September 1817 - The description of guards infantry **shakos** and **accouterments** and the instructions for the manner of wearing then, issued on this date, is also applied to the L.-Gds. Sapper Battalion [125].

8 December 1817 - It is ordered that for lower ranks the leather cuffs on cloth **pants** were to have spat-like extensions [*kozyr'ki*] [126].

23 August 1818 - The length and width of **shoulder straps** on tailcoats and greatcoats are defined, identical to that laid down at this time for Army and Guards Infantry and described above in detail for Grenadier regiments. It was also confirmed that musicians' and drummers' coats would have red shoulder wings or swallows' nests [*plechevye klapany ili kryl'tsa*] [127].

22 January 1819 - **Pompons** on miners' shakos, instead of the previous yellow, are ordered to be red, the same as for Sappers [128].

25 January 1819 - **Drumsticks** and the handles of **entrenching tools** are ordered to be be of mountain ash [*ryabinovoe derevo*], and lacquered [129].

4 April 1819 - For lower ranks the **spats** on the leggings were removed [130].

12 April 1819 - The **hornists** [*gornisty*] or **signalers** [*signalisty*] introduced onto the battalion's establishment are authorized the same uniform as for drummers, and the signal horns [*signalnye rozhki*] are to be of yellow brass, with white straps, and painted inside with black paint, with a gold wreath around the edge (Illus. 2209). In this same year all combatant ranks in the battalion, upon its transfer from the 2nd Guards Infantry Division to the 1st and in order to achieve uniformity with the other troops of this division, are ordered to have red flaps on the **cuffs** with white piping, while greatcoat collars were to be without tabs (Illus. 2209) [131].

20 September 1820 - Officers are given a new pattern **gorget**, identical to that received at this time by officers in the Guards Infantry and Guards Foot Artillery (Illus. 2210) [132]. In this same year there was a change for the dress coats of **musicians**, **signalers**, and **drummers**, consisting of the sewn-on chevrons beginning to be placed closer together than previously, almost touching one another, and on the swallows' nests the tape was no longer perpendicular as before, but at a diagonal toward the lower edge. Also, all four sides of the collar began to be trimmed with this tape (Illus. 2211) [133].

17 January 1822 - Lower ranks and officers are given round **pompons** for their shakos, for the former of red wool (Illus. 2211) and the latter of silver (Illus. 2212). Along with this, all these personnel are ordered to have red **turnbacks** on the coat skirts, with white piping (Illus. 2211 and 2212). Additionally, officers' **frock coats** were to have red linings [134].

26 November 1823 - All **musicians**, even though they might not hold non-commissioned officer ranks, are ordered to have: silver galloon on the coat and non-commisioned officers? pompons on the shakos. This does not apply to drummers if they do not hold non-commissioned officer rank [135].

16 January 1824 - The following changes are ordered in the uniforms and accouterments of combatant lower ranks:

1) **Coattails**, which up to this time had one covering the other, were to be cut so that their inner edges came together, and sewn together where they touched (Illus. 2213).

2.) To the decorative end [*trinchik*] of the **shako cords**, which is to be level with the right shoulder, is to be added a special loop of white cord attached to the button on the right shoulder strap, so that the shako cords will stay in place even when the soldier moved about (Illus. 2213).

3.) The **cartridge pouch** is to be worn so that when the soldier bends his elbow, the distance between it and a line level with the top edge of the pouch is to be equal to 3 vershoks [5-1/4 inches].

4.) The **knapsack** chest strap is to be fitted so that it passes between the third and fourth buttons of the coat, as counted from the bottom (Illus. 2213).

5.) On the **musket sling**, opposite the cocking piece, there is to be a loop of the same kind of leather as the sling, for stowing the flint cover [*ognivnyi chekhol*] when it has to be taken off (Illus. 2213) [136].

From this year, officers as well as lower ranks began to wear a taller **shako** with wider cords than previously (Illus. 2213), but no regulations were issued in this regard [137].

29 March 1825 - For combatant lower ranks, for faultless service, there were established **stripes** [*nashivki*] to be sewn on the left sleeve: for 10 years service - one, for 15 years - two, for 20 years - three; one over the other, all of yellow tape [138].

XLIII . GUARDS HORSE PIONEERS. *[Gvardeiskie konno-pionery.]*

28 November 1819 - The newly formed **L.-Gds. Horse-Pioneer Squadron** is ordered to have the same uniforms and shakos as the L.-Gds. Sapper Battalion, but with short skirts for the dress coats, and yellow pompons and simillarly colored pyramidal pompons. There are gray cloth taps on the greatcoat collar, and on the covers of officers' cartridge pouches an image of a two-headed eagel and two crossed axes. Saddlecloths are as for Guards Horse Artillery but with silver galloon for officers. All other uniform items, accouterments, and arms, as well as horse furniture, are as described above for the the 1st Horse-Pioneer Squadron (Illus. 2214, 2215, 2216, and 2217). When not on duty, officers are allowed to be in undress coats [*vitse-mundiry*] with long skirts (Illus. 2218) and the same frock coats [*syurtuki*] as possessed by officers in the L.-Gds. Sapper Battalion, but with white lining [139].

6 April 1822 - All combatant personnel in the squadron are ordered to have red **skirt turnbacks** with white piping instead of black with red, after the example established on 17 January of this year for the L.-Gds. Sapper Battalion (Illus. 2219) [140].

1 May 1824 - The pyramidal **pompons** on shakos are replaced by round ones. In this same year all combatant ranks began to wear a taller **shako** with wider cords. The latter had a special loop to attach to the button of the right shoulder strap (Illus. 2220) [141].

29 March 1825 - For combatant lower ranks, for faultless service, there are established **stripes** [*nashivki*] to be sewn on the left sleeve: for 10 years service - one, for 15 years - two, for 20 years - three; one over the other, all of yellow tape [142].

XLV . GUARDS ENGINEERS. *[Gvardeiskie inzhenery.]*

3 December 1820 - Field and company-grade officers of the **Guards Engineers** are ordered to wear the uniform prescribed for Field Engineers [*Polevye Inzenery*, i.e. ordinary Army engineers - M.C.] in these ranks, but with the addition of a silver edge to the collar, cuffs, and cuff flaps, the last items being red (Illus. 2221), and with silver Guards stars on the shabracks [143].

XLVI . GUARDS GENERAL STAFF. *[Gvardeiskii Generalnyi Shtab.]*

1 August 1814 - Generals and field and company-grade officers of the newly established **Guards General Staff** are ordered to have the exact same uniform as HIS IMPERIAL MAJESTY's Suite for Quartermaster Affairs has at this time, but with the addition of an embroidered gold edge on the collar and cuffs of the dress coat (Illus. 2222) [144].

10 July 1816 - These same ranks are ordered to have **silver appointments** instead of gold, instead of cavalry cuffs—infantry cuffs with red cloth flaps on which was three silver rows of the previous embroidery tracery, and instead of red cloth piping on the contre-epaulettes or cross straps [*kontr-epolet ili pogonchiki*]—black velvet piping (Illus. 2223 and 2224) [145].

7 March 1817 - All these ranks, instead of a double-breasted coat, are ordered to wear a **single-breasted coat** with nine buttons, with red cloth piping around the entire collar, on the cuffs, down the front opening, and on the pocket flaps. Also, instead of one **epaulette**, they are to have two, keeping the **aiguillette**, while **hats** were to be worn cocked fore-and-aft [*shlyapy nadevat's polya*] (Illus. 2225) [146].

▲ *The Prince general Koutousow at the battle of Toroutino the 6 October 1812*

NOTES

(1) Complete Collection of Laws [*Polnoe Sobranie Zakonov*, henceforth PSZ], Vol. XXVI, pg. 609, No. 19,826.

(2) Ibid., Vol. XLIV, Pt. II, regulation on uniforms, pg. 28, No. 19,863.

(3) Ibid., No. 19,867, and contemporary drawings and uniforms.

(4) Memorandum from the Commissariat Office to the Inspector of All Artillery, 11 June 1801.

(5) PSZ Vol. XLIV, pg. 30, No. 20,485, and information received from the War Ministry's Commissariat Department.

(6) Ibid., Vol. XLIV, pg. 28, No. 20,201.

(7) From the files of the War Ministry's Commissariat Department.

(8) From the same files, and drawings held in the SOVEREIGN EMPEROR'S Own Library, catalogued under No. 54.

(9) HIGHEST Confirmed table of uniforms and other items for the L.-Gds. Artillery Battalion, 17 December 1803; the drawings mentioned in the previous note, and information from contemporaries.

(10) Correspondence from the Inspector of All Artillery to the Commissariat Commission, 4 January 1805.

(11) From the files of the War Ministry's Commissariat Department.

(12) Drawings depicting various items of clothing and accouterments of Artillery crewmen, in the office of the Inspector of All Artillery, Graf Arakcheev, issued in 1807, and information from contemporaries.

(13) From the files of the War Ministry's Commissariat Department.

(14) From the files of that same Department

(15) Statements by contemporaries.

(16) PSZ Vol. XLIV, pgs. 14, No. 22,633 and 13, No. 22,720, and from the files of the War Ministry's Commissariat Department.

(17) PSZ Vol. XLIV, pg. 13, No. 22,727, from the files of the same Department, and statements by contemporaries.

(18) Signed Ukase announced to the Military Collegium by the Minister of Military Land Forces, 3 January 1808, and from the files of the War Ministry's Commissariat Department.

(19) PSZ Vol. XX, pg. 45, No. 22,784, and statements from contemporaries.

(20) From the files of the War Ministry's Commissariat Department, and actual shakos preserved up to the present time.

(21) File from the archive of the War Ministry's Inspection Department, with drawings and a description of how to wear the knapsack and greatcoat, 1808, No. 13786/654, from the files of the War Ministry's Commissariat Department, statements from contemporaries.

(22) PSZ Vol. XLIV, pg. 67, No. 23,335.

(23) Ibid., Vol. XXX, pg. 669, No. 23,343.

(24) From the files of the War Ministry's Commissariat Department.

(25) PSZ Vol. XLIV, pg. 13, No. 23,548.

(26) From the files of the War Ministry's Commissariat Department, and contemporary drawings and uniforms.

(27) From the files of the same Department.

(28) PSZ Vol. XXX, pg. 950, No. 23,625, and from the files of the War Ministry's Commissariat Department.

(29) PSZ Vol. XXX, pg. 965, No. 23,654.

(30) Ibid., pg. 1006, No. 23,695.

(31) Ibid., Vol. XLIV, pg. 31 No. 22,373, and model pattern shako cords preserved in the War Ministry's Commissariat Department.

(32) From the files of the War Ministry's Commissariat Department, and statements from contemporaries.

(33) Ditto.

(34) Ditto.

(35) PSZ Vol. XXXI, pg. 362, No.24,357.

(36) Ibid., pg. 517, No. 24,488, and from the files of the War Ministry's Commissariat Department.

(37) From the files of the War Ministry's Commissariat Department.

(38) Ditto.

(39) Statements from contemporaries.

(40) From the files of the War Ministry's Commissariat Department.

(41) Ditto.

(42) Ditto.

(43) PSZ Vol. XLIV, pg. 103, No. 25,592.

(44) From the files of the War Ministry's Commissariat Department, and statements by contemporaries.

(45) PSZ Vol. XXXIII, pg. 103, No. 26,037.

(46) Ibid., Vol. XXXIII, pg. 450, No. 26,095, and from the files of the War Ministry's Commissariat Department.

(47) Highest Confirmed description of the uniforms for Guards Artillery, 12 May 1817, and from the files of the War

Ministry's Commissariat Department.
(48) From the files of that same Department.
(49) Ditto.
(50) PSZ, Vol. XLIV, pg. 120.
(51) From the files of the War Ministry's Commissariat Department.
(52) Ditto.
(53) Ditto.
(54) PSZ Vol. XLIV, pg. 104, No. 27,298.
(55) Ibid., Vol. XLIV, pg. 102, No. 27,311.
(56) Ibid., pg. 121 and 122, No.27,504, and from the files of the War Ministry's Commissariat Department.
(57) Ditto.
(58) PSZ Vol. XLIV, pg. 108 No. 27,653.
(59) Order of the Chief of H.I.M.'s Main Staff, 4 April 1818, No. 21.
(60) From the files of the War Ministry's Commissariat Department, and statements by contemporaries.
(61) From the files of that same Department and contemporary drawings and uniforms.
(62) PSZ, Vol. XLIV, pg. 122, No. 29,658.
(63) Order to the Separate Corps of Military Settlements, 16 January 1824, No. 22, and contemporary drawings and uniforms.
(64) Contemporary drawings and shakos.
(65) PSZ Vol. XL, pg. 188, No. 30,309.
(66) Ibid., Vol. XXVI, pg. 609, No. 19, 826.
(67) Ibid., Vol. XLIV, pg. 28, No. 19,863.
(68) Ibid., Vol. XLIV, pg. 15, No. 19,867, and contemporary drawings.
(69) Memorandum from the Commissariat Office to the Inspector of All Artillery, 11 June 1801.
(70) PSZ., Vol. XLIV, pg. 14 No. 20,204.
(71) Ibid., pg. 30, No. 20,485, and from the files of the War Ministry's Commissariat Department.
(72) Ibid., pg. 28, No. 20,201.
(73) Ibid., Vol. XXVII, pg. 934, No. 20,989; from the files of the War Ministry's Commissariat Department; drawings held in the SOVEREIGN EMPEROR'S Own Library, catalogued under No. 54.
(74) Proposal by the Intendant-General of the Army to the Commissariat Office, 17 December 1803.
(75) Highest confirmed table of uniforms and accouterments for the L.-Gds. Artillery Regiment's Horse Company, 17 December 1803, and from the files of the War Ministry's Commissariat Department.
(76) Statements from contemporaries and contemporary drawings.
(77) Proposal of the Intendant-General of the Army to the Commissariat Office, 27 February 1804.
(78) From the files of the War Ministry?s Commissariat Department.
(79) The drawings referenced above under Note 12, and from the files of the War Ministry's Commissariat Department.
(80) From the files of the War Ministry's Commissariat Department.
(81) Ditto.
(82) Statements from contemporaries.
(83) Signed Ukase relayed to the Military Collegium by the Minister for Military Land Forces, 3 January 1808, and from the files of the War Ministry's Commissariat Department.
(84) PSZ Vol. XXX, pg. 45, No. 22,784, and statements by contemporaries.
(85) Ibid., Vol. XLIV, pg. 13, No. 23,373, and pg. 54, No. 23,373.
(86) Ibid., Vol. XLIV, pg. 13, No. 23,548.
(87) From the files of the War Ministry's Commissariat Department.
(88) Ditto.
(89) PSZ Vol. XXX, pg. 1006, No. 23,695.
(90) Ibid., Vol. XLIV, pg. 28, No. 23,925, and fromthe files of the War Ministry's Commissariat Department.
(91) Statements by contemporaries.
(92) From the files of the War Ministry's Commissariat Department, and contemporary uniform coats and other items.
(93) From the files of the same Department.
(94) Statements by contemporaries.
(95) From the files of the War Ministry's Commissariat Department, and statements from contemporaries.
(96) From the files of the same Department.
(97) Ditto.

(98) Ditto.

(99) Statements by contemporaries.

(100) HIGHEST Directive sent by HIS IMPERIAL HIGHNESS THE TSAREVICH to the acting head of the War Ministry, 7 March 1816, No. 143.

(101) PSZ Vol. XLIV, pg. 120, No. 26,789.

(102) From the files of the War Ministry's Commissariat Department.

(103) PSZ Vol. XLIV, pg. 102, No. 27,311.

(104) Ibid., pg. 104, No. 27,298.

(105) Proposal by the Minister for War to the Commissariat Department, 18 March 1818, No. 1227.

(106) PSZ Vol. XLIV, pg. 102, No. 27,311.

(107) Ibid., pg. 101, No. 27,681.

(108) Ibid., pg. 102, No. 28,251.

(109) From the files of the War Ministry's Commissariat Department, and contemporary drawings and uniforms.

(110) PSZ Vol. XLIV, pg. 103, No. 29,888.

(111) Contemporary drawings and shakos.

(112) PSZ Vol. XL, pg. 188, No. 30,309.

(113) From the files of the War Ministry's Commissariat Department; uniforms and other items preserved up to the present time, and statements from contemporaries.

(114) From the files of the War Ministry's Commissariat Department.

(115) PSZ Vol. XXXII, pg. 844, No. 25,627.

(116) From the files of the War Ministry's Commissariat Department, and statements from contemporaries.

(117) PSZ Vol. XXXIII, pg. 450, No.26,095, and *Collection of Laws and Regulations Relating to the Military Administration*, 1816, Book I, pgs. 81 and 82.

(118) Signed Ukase relayed by the acting head of the War Ministry to the Inspection Department, 5 March 1816, No. 142.

(119) Table of 9 March 1816.

(120) PSZ Vol. XXXIII, pg. 854, No. 26,281.

(121) Ibid., Vol. XLIV, pg. 104, No. 26,842.

(122) Confirmed description of the uniform for the L.-Gds. Sapper Btg, 12 May 1817, and contemporary uniforms.

(123) PSZ Vol. XLIV, pg. 120.

(124) Ibid., pg. 104, No. 26,992.

(125) Ibid., pg. 104, No. 27,067.

(126) From the files of the War Ministry's Commissariat Department.

(127) PSZ Vol. XLIV, pgs. 121 and 122, No. 27,504, and from the files of the War Ministry's Commissariat Department.

(128) Ibid., pg. 116, No. 27,449.

(129) Ibid., pg. 108, No. 27,653.

(130) From the files of the War Ministry's Commissariat Department, and contemporary drawings.

(131) Ditto.

(132) Ditto.

(133) From the same files and contemporary uniforms.

(134) PSZ, Vol. XLIV, pg. 103, No. 28,874.

(135) Ibid., pg. 122, No. 29,658.

(136) Order to the Separate Corps of Military Settlements, 16 January 1824, No. 22, and contemporary drawings and uniforms.

(137) Contemporary drawings and shakos.

(138) PSZ Vol. XL, pg. 188 No. 30,309.

(139) From the files of the War Ministry's Commissariat Department, contemporary drawings, and contemporary uniforms and other items.

(140) PSZ Vol. XLIV, pg. 102, No. 28,992.

(141) Ibid., pg. 103, No. 29,888.

(142) Ibid., Vol. XL, pg. 188, No. 30,309.

(143) From the files of the War Ministry's Commissariat Department; contemporary drawings and uniforms and statements from contemporaries.

(144) Ditto.

(145) Ditto.

(146) Ditto.

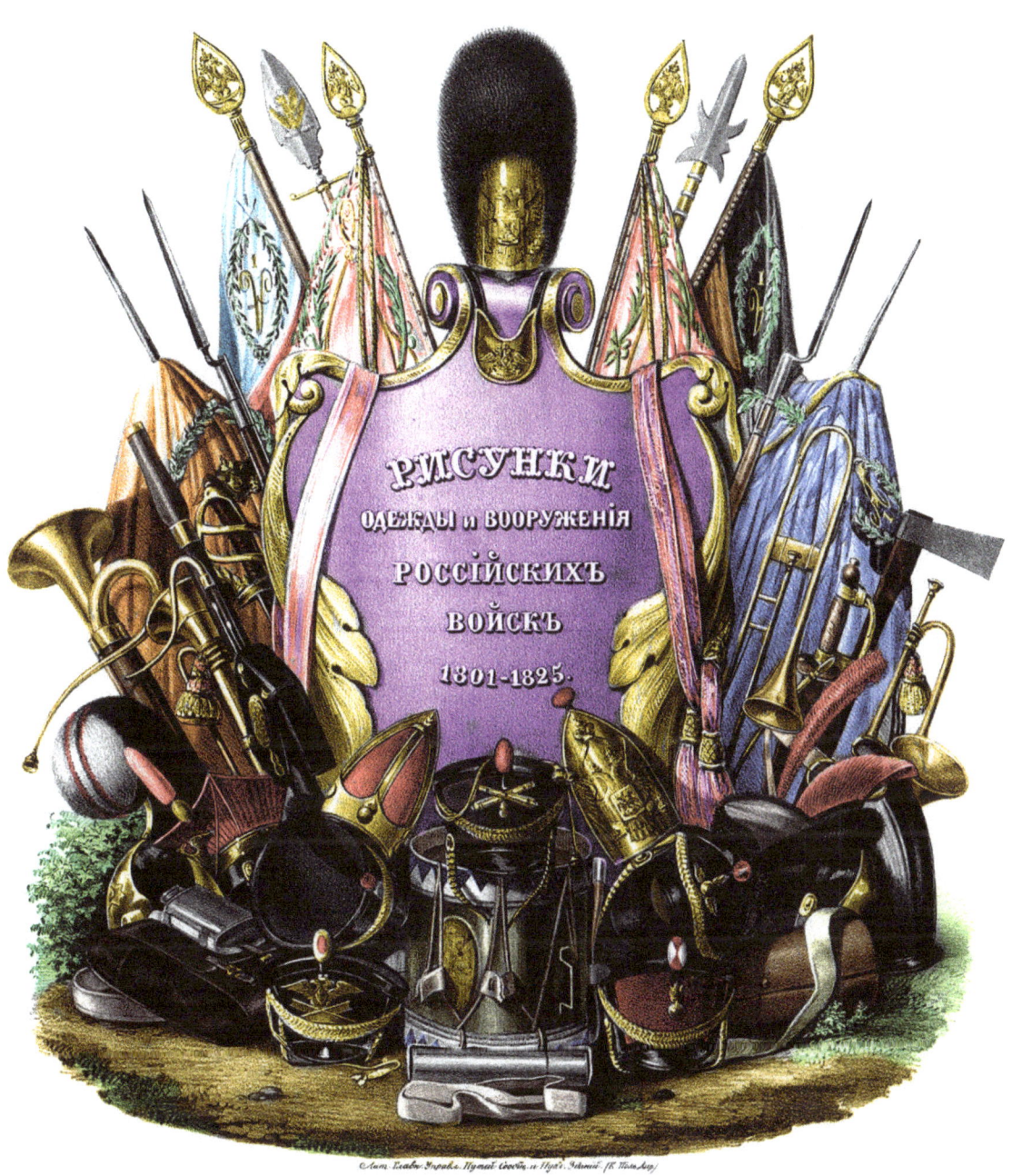

РИСУНКИ
ОДЕЖДЫ и ВООРУЖЕНІЯ
РОССІЙСКИХЪ
ВОЙСКЪ
1801-1825.

PLATES LIST OF ILLUSTRATIONS

2170. Company-Grade Officer. 2nd Guards Artillery Brigade, 1820-1824.

2171. Musicians. 1st Guards Artillery Brigade, 1820-1824.

2172. Non-Commissioned Officers [*Feierverkery*]. 1st and 2nd Guards Artillery Brigades, 1824-1825.

2173. Company-Grade Officer. 1st Guards Artillery Brigade, 1824-1825.

2174. Bombardier and Company-Grade Officer. Guards Horse Artillery, 1801-1802. *Note. In the same year of 1802, straw-colored gloves and netherwear were replaced by white.*

2175. Company-Grade Officer. L.-Gds. Horse Artillery, 1802-1803.

2176. Bombardier. Guards Horse Artillery, 1803-1807.

2177. Cannoneer and Trumpeter. Guards Horse Artillery, 1803-1807.

2178. Non-Commissioned Officer [*Feierverker*]. Guards Horse Artillery, 1803-1807.

2179. Company-Grade Officer. Guards Horse Artillery, 1803-1807.

2180. Company-Grade Officer. Guards Horse Artillery, 1803-1807.

2181. Cannoneer. Guards Horse Artillery, 1806-1807.

2182. Field-Grade Officer. Guards Horse Artillery, 1807-1809.

2183. Field-Grade Officer. Guards Horse Artillery, 1809-1811.

2184. Company-Grade Officers. Guards Horse Artillery, 1808-1811. *(In campaign and parade uniform.)*

2185. Cannoneer. Guards Horse Artillery, 1808-1809.

2186. Cannoneer. Guards Horse Artillery, 1809-1811.

2187. Non-Commissioned Officer [*Feierverker*] and Cannoneer. Guards Horse Artillery, 1811-1812.

2188. Trumpeter and Company-Grade Officer. Guards Horse Artillery, 1811.

2189. Cannoneer. Guards Horse Artillery, 1812-1814.

2190. Company-Grade Officer. Guards Horse Artillery, 1812-1824.

2191-92. Company-Grade Officer and Non-Commissioned Officer. Guards Horse Artillery, 1814-1817.

2193. Bombardier. Guards Horse Artillery, 1817-1820.

2194. Company-Grade Officers. Guards Horse Artillery, 1817-1819.

2195. Officer's Cartridge Pouch for the Guards Horse Artillery, established in 1817.

2196. Cannoneer and Company-Grade Officer. L.-Gds. Horse Light Battery No. 3, 1818-1820.

2197. Company-Grade Officer and Cannoneer. Guards Horse Artillery, 1818-1820.

2198. Trumpeter and Company-Grade Officer. Guards Horse Artillery, 1820-1824.

2199. Company-Grade Officer and Bombardier. Guards Horse Artillery, 1824-1825.

2200. Miner. L.-Gds. Sapper Battalion, 1812-1814.

2201. Sapper and Non-Commissioned Officer. L.-Gds. Sapper Battalion, 1812-1815.

2202. Musician and Field-Grade Officer. L.-Gds. Sapper Battalion, 1812-1815.

2203. Miner. L.-Gds. Sapper Battalion, 1814-1815.

2204. Non-Commissioned Officer and Miner. L.-Gds. Sapper Battalion, 1816-1817.

2205. Shako Plate for the L.-Gds. Sapper Battalion, established 1816.

2206. Field-Grade Officer and Company-Grade Officer. L.-Gds. Sapper Battalion, 1816-1817.

2207. Miner. L.-Gds. Sapper Battalion, 1817-1819.

2208. Adjutant. L.-Gds. Sapper Battalion, 1817-1820.

2209. Signaler [*Signalist*]. L.-Gds. Sapper Battalion, 1820-1822.

2210. Company-Grade Officer. L.-Gds. Sapper Battalion, 1820-1822.

2211. Private and Drummer. L.-Gds. Sapper Battalion, 1822-1824.

2212. Company-Grade Officer. L.-Gds. Sapper Battalion, 1822-1824.

2213. Private, Non-Commissioned Officer, and Company-Grade Officer. L.-Gds. Sapper Battalion, 1824-1825.

2214. Private. L.-Gds. Horse-Pioneer Squadron, 1819-1824.

2215. Non-Commissioned Officer and Trumpeter. L.-Gds. Horse-Pioneer Squadron, 1819-1824.

2216. Field-Grade Officer. L.-Gds. Horse-Pioneer Squadron, 1822-1824

2217. Officer's Cartridge Pouch,. L.-Gds. Horse-Pioneer Squadron, since 1819.

2218. Company-Grade Officers. L-Gds. Horse-Pioneer Squadron, 1819-1825. Note: In 1822, the coattail turnbacks were ordered to be red with white piping instead of black with red.

2219. Field-Grade Officer and Non-Commissioned Officer. L.-Gds. Horse-Pioneer Squadron, 1822-1824.

2220. Private and Company-Grade Officer. L.-Gds. Horse-Pioneer Squadron, 1824-1825.

2221. Field-Grade Officer. Guards Engineers, 1820-1825.

2222. Company-Grade Officer. Guards General Staff, 1814-1816.

2223. Company-Grade Officer. Guards General Staff, 1816-1817.

2224. Officers' Embroidery for the Guards General Staff, since 1816.

2225. Field-Grade Officer. Guards General Staff, 1817-1825.

2138

Company-Grade Officer and Cannoneer. Guards Foot Artillery, 1801-1803.

25

Officer's shabrack and pistol carriers of the Guards Foot Artillery, established in 1803.

Mounted-Gun Handler, Bombardier, and Cannoneer. Guards Foot Artillery, 1803-1807.

Non-Commmissioned Officer [Feierverker] and Drummer. Guards Foot Artillery, 1803-1807.

Field-Grade Officer and Company-Grade Officer. Guards Foot Artillery, 1803-1807.

Bombardier and Cannoneer. Guards Foot Artillery, 1805-1807.

Company-Grade Officer. Guards Foot Artillery, 1807-1809.

Non-Commmissioned Officer [Feierverker] and Cannoneer. Guards Foot Artillery, 1807-1808. (In winter and summer uniform.)

Non-Commmissioned Officer [Feierverker] and Bombardier. Guards Foot Artillery, 1808-1809.

Shako plate for Guards Foot Artillery, established 1808. Shako plate for Guards Foot Artillery, established in 1817. Shako Plate for the L.-Gds. Sapper Battalion, established 1816.

Company-Grade Officer and General. Guards Foot Artillery, 1808-1809.

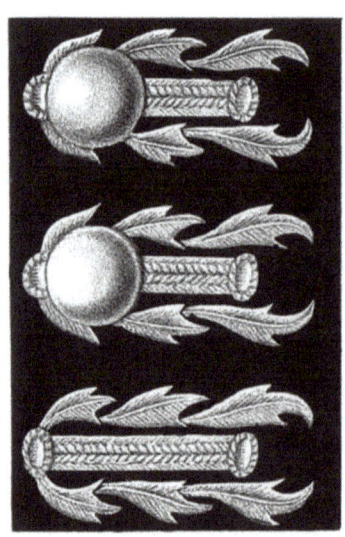

Officers' embroidery for Guards Artillery, established in 1809.

Cannoneer and Non-Commmissioned Officer [Feierverker]. Guards Foot Artillery, 1809-1810.

Field-Grade Officer and General. Guards Foot Artillery, 1809.

Cannoneer and Non-Commmissioned Officer [Feierverker]. Guards Foot Artillery, 1809-1810.

Company-Grade Officer. Guards Foot Artillery, 1809-1810.

Bombardier. Guards Foot Artillery, 1810-1811.

Company-Grade Officers. Guards Foot Artillery, 1810-1811.

Non-Commmissioned Officers [Feierverkery]. Guards Foot Artillery, 1811.

Company-Grade Officer and Bombardier. Guards Foot Artillery, 1812-1814.

Non-Combatants. Guards Foot Artillery, 1812-1825.

Company-Grade Officer. Guards Foot Artillery, 1814-1816.

Non-Commmissioned Officer [Feierverker], Bombardier, and Drummer. Guards Foot Artillery, 1814-1816.

Cannoneer and Company-Grade Officer. 1st Guards Artillery Brigade, 1817-1818.

Drum Major. 1st Guards Artillery Brigade, 1817-1818.

Field-Grade Officer and Bombardier. 2nd Guards Artillery Brigade, 1817-1824.

Drummer and Musician. 2nd Guards Artillery Brigade, 1817-1824.

Company-Grade Officer of the 1st and Non-Commissioned Officer of the 2nd Guards Artillery Brigades, 1817-1824.

Bombardier. L.-Gds. Foot Battery Company No. 5, 1818-1824.

Field-Grade Officer. L.-Gds. Foot Battery Company No. 5, 1818-1824.

Company-Grade Officer and Cannoneer. 1st Guards Artillery Brigade, 1818-1824.

2170

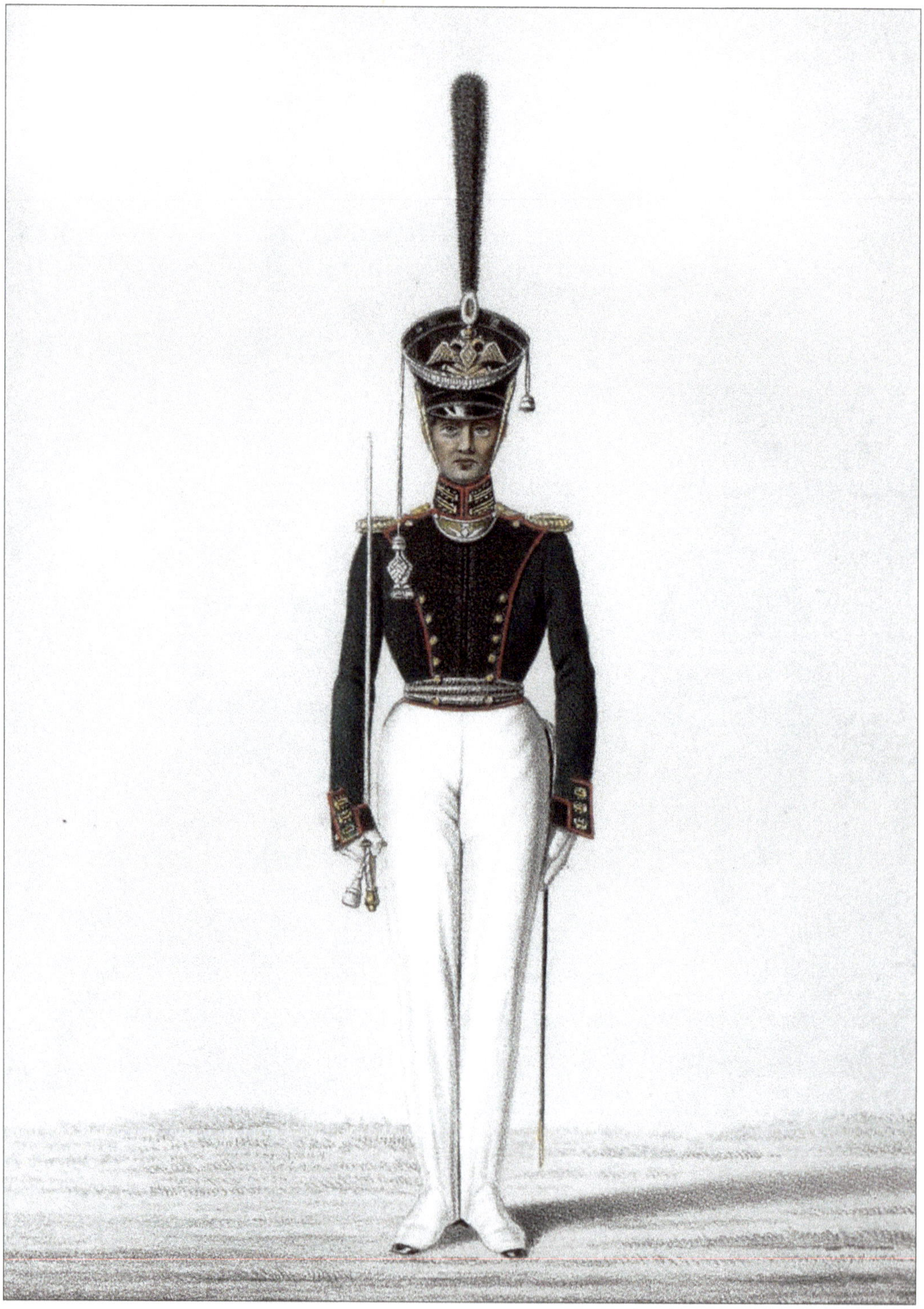

Company-Grade Officer. 2nd Guards Artillery Brigade, 1820-1824.

Musicians. 1st Guards Artillery Brigade, 1820-1824.

Non-Commissioned Officers [Feierverkery]. 1st and 2nd Guards Artillery Brigades, 1824-1825.

Company-Grade Officer. 1st Guards Artillery Brigade, 1824-1825.

Bombardier and Company-Grade Officer. Guards Horse Artillery, 1801-1802.

Company-Grade Officer. L.-Gds. Horse Artillery, 1802-1803.

Bombardier. Guards Horse Artillery, 1803-1807.

Cannoneer and Trumpeter. Guards Horse Artillery, 1803-1807.

Non-Commissioned Officer [Feierverker]. Guards Horse Artillery, 1803-1807.

2179

Company-Grade Officer. Guards Horse Artillery, 1803-1807.

Company-Grade Officer. Guards Horse Artillery, 1803-1807.

Cannoneer. Guards Horse Artillery, 1806-1807.

Field-Grade Officer. Guards Horse Artillery, 1807-1809.

Field-Grade Officer. Guards Horse Artillery, 1809-1811.

Company-Grade Officers. Guards Horse Artillery, 1808-1811. (In campaign and parade uniform.)

Cannoneer. Guards Horse Artillery, 1808-1809.

Cannoneer. Guards Horse Artillery, 1809-1811.

Non-Commissioned Officer [Feierverker] and Cannoneer. Guards Horse Artillery, 1811-1812.

Trumpeter and Company-Grade Officer. Guards Horse Artillery, 1811.

Cannoneer. Guards Horse Artillery, 1812-1814.

Company-Grade Officer. Guards Horse Artillery, 1812-1824.

Company-Grade Officer and Non-Commissioned Officer. Guards Horse Artillery, 1814-1817.

Bombardier. Guards Horse Artillery, 1817-1820.

Company-Grade Officers. Guards Horse Artillery, 1817-1819.

Officer's Cartridge Pouch for the Guards Horse Artillery, established in 1817.

Cannoneer and Company-Grade Officer. L.-Gds. Horse Light Battery No. 3, 1818-1820.

Company-Grade Officer and Cannoneer. Guards Horse Artillery, 1818-1820.

Trumpeter and Company-Grade Officer. Guards Horse Artillery, 1820-1824.

Company-Grade Officer and Bombardier. Guards Horse Artillery, 1824-1825.

Miner. L.-Gds. Sapper Battalion, 1812-1814.

Sapper and Non-Commissioned Officer. L.-Gds. Sapper Battalion, 1812-1815.

Musician and Field-Grade Officer. L.-Gds. Sapper Battalion, 1812-1815.

Miner. L.-Gds. Sapper Battalion, 1814-1815.

Non-Commissioned Officer and Miner. L.-Gds. Sapper Battalion, 1816-1817.

Field-Grade Officer and Company-Grade Officer. L.-Gds. Sapper Battalion, 1816-1817.

Miner. L.-Gds. Sapper Battalion, 1817-1819.

Adjutant. L.-Gds. Sapper Battalion, 1817-1820.

Signaler [Signalist]. L.-Gds. Sapper Battalion, 1820-1822.

Company-Grade Officer. L.-Gds. Sapper Battalion, 1820-1822.

Private and Drummer. L.-Gds. Sapper Battalion, 1822-1824.

Company-Grade Officer. L.-Gds. Sapper Battalion, 1822-1824.

Private, Non-Commissioned Officer, and Company-Grade Officer. L.-Gds. Sapper Battalion, 1824-1825

Private. L.-Gds. Horse-Pioneer Squadron, 1819-1824.

Non-Commissioned Officer and Trumpeter. L.-Gds. Horse-Pioneer Squadron, 1819-1824.

Field-Grade Officer. L.-Gds. Horse-Pioneer Squadron, 1822-1824

Officer's Cartridge Pouch, L.-Gds. Horse-Pioneer Squadron, since 1819.

Company-Grade Officers. L-Gds. Horse-Pioneer Squadron, 1819-1825.

Field-Grade Officer and Non-Commissioned Officer. L.-Gds. Horse-Pioneer Squadron, 1822-1824.

Private and Company-Grade Officer. L.-Gds. Horse-Pioneer Squadron, 1824-1825.

Field-Grade Officer. Guards Engineers, 1820-1825.

Company-Grade Officer. Guards General Staff, 1814-1816.

Company-Grade Officer. Guards General Staff, 1816-1817.

Officers' Embroidery for the Guards General Staff, since 1816.

Field-Grade Officer. Guards General Staff, 1817-1825.

SOLDIERS, WEAPONS & UNIFORMS ALREADY PUBLISHED
(SOME TITLES)

UNIFORMS OF RUSSIAN ARMY IN THE ERA OF ANCIENT TZAR
FROM THE REIGN OF VASILI IV TO MICHAEL I, ALEXIS, FEODOR III DURING THE XVII th CENTURY
A.V.VISKOVATOV — LUCA STEFANO CRISTINI
SWU-600-004

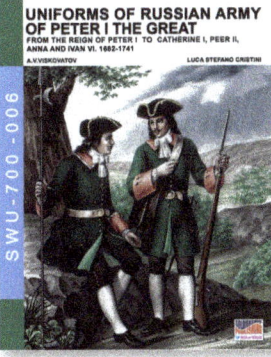

UNIFORMS OF RUSSIAN ARMY OF PETER I THE GREAT
FROM THE REIGN OF PETER I TO CATHERINE I, PEER II, ANNA AND IVAN VI. 1682-1741
A.V.VISKOVATOV — LUCA STEFANO CRISTINI
SWU-700-006

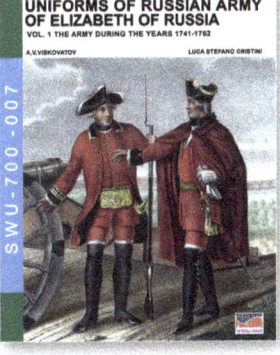

UNIFORMS OF RUSSIAN ARMY OF ELIZABETH OF RUSSIA
VOL. 1 THE ARMY DURING THE YEARS 1741-1762
A.V.VISKOVATOV — LUCA STEFANO CRISTINI
SWU-700-007

UNIFORMS OF RUSSIAN ARMY OF ELIZABETH OF RUSSIA
VOL. 2 THE ARMY DURING THE YEARS 1741-1762
A.V.VISKOVATOV — LUCA STEFANO CRISTINI
SWU-700-008

UNIFORMS OF RUSSIAN ARMY IN THE XVIII CENTURY VOL. 1
UNDER THE REIGN OF CATHERINE II EMPRESS OF RUSSIA BETWEEN 1762 AND 1796
A.V.VISKOVATOV — LUCA STEFANO CRISTINI
SWU-700-005

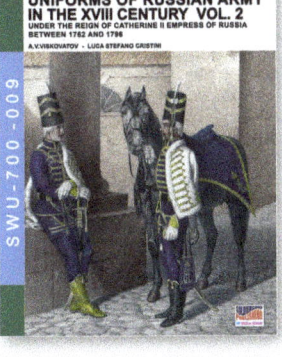

UNIFORMS OF RUSSIAN ARMY IN THE XVIII CENTURY VOL. 2
UNDER THE REIGN OF CATHERINE II EMPRESS OF RUSSIA BETWEEN 1762 AND 1796
A.V.VISKOVATOV — LUCA STEFANO CRISTINI
SWU-700-009

UNIFORMS OF RUSSIAN ARMY IN THE XVIII CENTURY VOL. 3
UNDER THE REIGN OF CATHERINE II EMPRESS OF RUSSIA BETWEEN 1762 AND 1796
A.V.VISKOVATOV — LUCA STEFANO CRISTINI
SWU-700-010

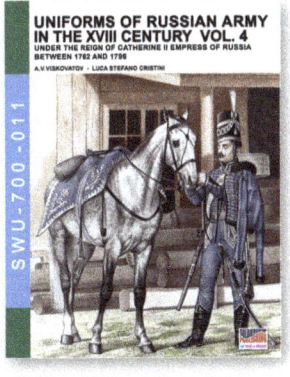

UNIFORMS OF RUSSIAN ARMY IN THE XVIII CENTURY VOL. 4
UNDER THE REIGN OF CATHERINE II EMPRESS OF RUSSIA BETWEEN 1762 AND 1796
A.V.VISKOVATOV — LUCA STEFANO CRISTINI
SWU-700-011

BRITISH ARMY UNIFORMS IN 1742
IN THE ART OF JOHN PINE
SWU-700-001

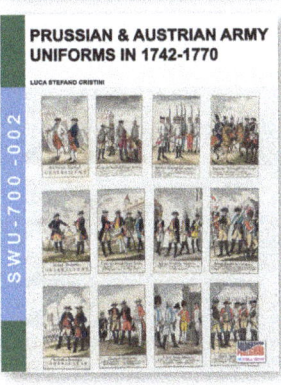

PRUSSIAN & AUSTRIAN ARMY UNIFORMS IN 1742-1770
LUCA STEFANO CRISTINI
SWU-700-002

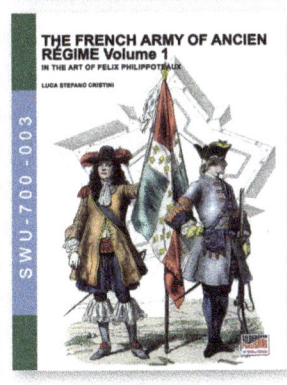

THE FRENCH ARMY OF ANCIEN RÉGIME Volume 1
IN THE ART OF FELIX PHILIPPOTEAUX
LUCA STEFANO CRISTINI
SWU-700-003

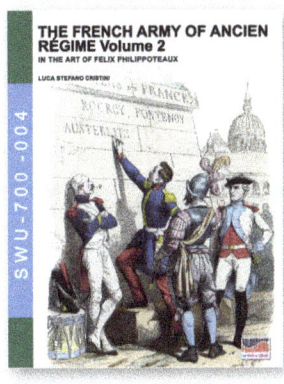

THE FRENCH ARMY OF ANCIEN RÉGIME Volume 2
IN THE ART OF FELIX PHILIPPOTEAUX
LUCA STEFANO CRISTINI
SWU-700-004

THE EXERCISE OF ARMES
JACOB DE GHEYN II — LUCA S. CRISTINI
SWU-600-001

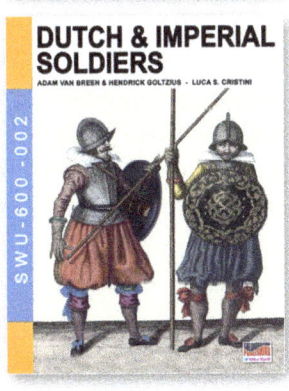

DUTCH & IMPERIAL SOLDIERS
ADAM VAN BREEN & HENDRICK GOLTZIUS — LUCA S. CRISTINI
SWU-600-002

HORSEMEN IN THE 16TH & 17TH C.
JACOB DE GHEYN II — A. DE BRUYN — LUCA S. CRISTINI
SWU-600-003

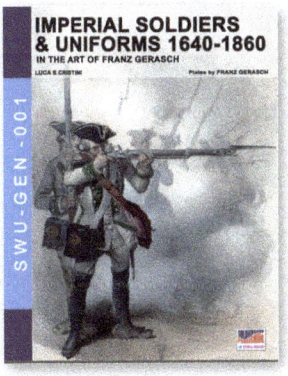

IMPERIAL SOLDIERS & UNIFORMS 1640-1860
IN THE ART OF FRANZ GERASCH
LUCA S. CRISTINI   Plates by FRANZ GERASCH
SWU-GEN-001